# Beyond

## Where Our Limitations No Longer Matter

By
Rev. Brian Sharp

Beyond
© 2017 by Brian Sharp
Published by Timothy Publishing Services
3409 W Gary St
Broken Arrow, OK 74012

Unless otherwise identified, Scripture references are taken from the New International Version®, NIV® (1984), italics may be added for emphasis, © 1973, 1978, 1984, 2011 by Biblica, Inc.TM Used by permission. All rights reserved worldwide.

Scripture quotations marked (AMP) are taken from the Amplified Bible, Copyright © 1954, 1958, 1962, 1964, 1965, 1987 by the Lockman Foundation. Used by permission.

Scripture quotations marked (HCSB) are taken from the Holman Christian Standard Bible © 1999, 2000, 2002, 2003 by Holman Bible Publishers. Used by permission.

Scripture quotations marked (MSG) are taken from The Message© by Eugene H. Peterson, 1993, 1994, 1995 by Navpress Publishing Group. Used by Permission.

Scripture quotations marked (NET) are taken from the New English Translation, NET Bible® copyright ©1996-2016 by Biblical Studies Press, L.L.C. http://netbible.org. All rights reserved. Used by Permission.

Front cover photo of Helix Nebula courtesy of Hubble Space Telescope, STScI, NASA. Public Domain.

ISBN -13: 978-1-940931-18-0

Library of Congress catalog card number: 2017943617

# Table of Contents

# Introduction

When it comes to our walk with God through Jesus Christ, having comfort as our goal can be lethal. While God is certainly not against comfort, it can lead to complacency which is the breeding ground for all kinds of self-centeredness, not to mention stagnation of life and ministry. This book is about getting beyond where we presently are, by focusing on our loving God Who is beyond any and all limitations.

God has called each of us to a higher level of life where we can know His heart and do greater work for Him. This, however, is all dependent on how willing we are to move beyond our present condition. It is God's general practice not to cross the line of our human will. If we don't want more of Him, desire a deeper intimacy with Him, and yearn for a greater impact on our world, then He will let us remain where we are, but we will suffer the consequences.

He doesn't view us as robots, but the beloved crown of His creation. Thus, He desires above all else, that we be in a close, personal, actively-growing relationship with Him.

If you are totally satisfied with your life or ministry the way it is, then this book probably isn't for you. But if you desire to be and do more for the kingdom of God, then the pages of this book just might be a useful tool God will use to energize, or re-energize, your life and spiritual vision. With our "above and beyond" God as our source, our limitations are only opportunities for Him to show off!

## Chapter 1

# How Big is Your God?

Now to Him who is able to do above and beyond all that we ask or think according to the power that works in us. (Ephesians 3:20 HCSB)

When I was twelve years old I had a telescope. I would often just play with it looking at everything from my neighbor's house which was a quarter of a mile away, to Canadian geese in the corn field behind my farmhouse, to the moon and other various celestial bodies, which was my favorite way to use my telescope.

On one particularly clear night I had the moon focused in, filling up my lens with intricate detail—craters, large areas called "seas," and the like. My mother had given me an old camera that had a time-release shutter that would stay open as long as I held it. On a whim, I placed the camera on the telescope lens, held the shutter for a few seconds and took a picture. When I picked up the pictures from the drug store I couldn't wait to see if what I had done actually worked. To my surprise the picture turned out amazingly clear; a total fluke I was very proud of!

Another time, I was randomly picking out points of light in the night sky to look at. If you've had any experience with telescopes, then you know that stars don't come into sharp focus because they're gaseous balls of light. But on this particular evening I picked out one of the points of light, and as I focused it began to take on a certain shape. By the time it came into clear focus my mouth dropped open. I had found Saturn! There it was, a tiny ball with little rings around it. Out of the multiple thousands of points of light I could've chosen, I picked Saturn. What are the chances?

Super excited at my "discovery," I ran upstairs, woke my sister and yelled, "You've got to come down and look through my telescope, I found Saturn!" She reluctantly got up, put on her fuzzy house coat and slippers and trudged outside in forty degree temperatures. I re-centered my telescope on Saturn and told her to look. She put her eye on the lens and said, "That's neat. Can I go back to bed now?" I said,

"Sure," not understanding why she didn't share my excitement for this truly amazing event.

The intrigue for me was that I was able to look beyond what my naked eye could see. I had a desire to look further than my natural senses could perceive, because I knew there was more "out there." Since then, I've learned that no matter how much of the universe scientists have seen or discovered there's always more, and always will be.

Even though I grew up and went on to other things I have never lost my interest in outer space and the magnificence of God's universe. The nearly unbelievable sizes and astronomical numbers needed to express distances are testament to the grandeur of God.

Take, for instance, the picture of the Helix Nebula, NGC 7293 on the front of this book. It is a high-resolution, infra-red photo captured by the Hubble Space Telescope from NASA. I dubbed it the "eye of God" the first time I saw it, long before I realized others have described it like this, for good reason. It is 650 light-years from earth and 2.5 to 3 light years from end to end. If you're not into astronomy this might not mean much to you, so let's put some perspective on this.

- The speed of light travels at 186,000 miles per second. If you could travel at this rate you would circum-navigate the equator approximately 7.5 times in one second!

- Our sun is 93,000,000 miles from earth. It takes light approximately 8 minutes and 20 seconds to reach earth.

- To go from one end of Helix Nebula to the other...

  Multiply 31,536,000 seconds in a year by 2.5 years and you get 78,840,000 seconds in two and a half years (31,536,000 X 2.5 = 78,840,000).

  Then multiply 78,840,000 by 186,000 miles per second and you get the number of miles across Helix Nebula. It was precisely at this point my handy, dandy little calculator couldn't handle it. It read 1.46642e13.

Please understand I am not a math whiz nor do I have a doctorate in astronomy, but I do know this is one super-huge number that is extremely difficult for most of us to comprehend. And to think that this is just one of a countless number of nebulas, stars, planets, solar systems, galaxies, pulsars, black holes and a myriad of other celestial members of God's creation!

The same is true when we go in the other direction and examine the minutest details of His earthly creation, especially humans. Microscopes take us into quite another world of cells, genes, chromosomes, atoms, protons, neutrons, electrons, sub-atomic particles, etc. All this only reinforces the unavoidable realities of both the greatness of our

God and the idea there's more, so much more than we've yet discovered and experienced.

> How great is God—beyond our understanding! The number of His years is past finding out. (Job 36:26)

> God's voice thunders in marvelous ways; He does great things beyond our understanding. (Job 37:5)

> As the heavens are higher than the earth, so are my ways higher than your ways and my thoughts than your thoughts. (Isaiah 55:9)

> The Lord wraps himself in light as with a garment; He stretches out the heavens like a tent and lays the beams of His upper chambers on their waters. He makes the clouds His chariot and rides on the wings of the wind. (Psalm 104:2-3)

> Great is the Lord and most worthy of praise; His greatness no one can fathom. (Psalm 145:3)

> …and on and on it goes…

As human beings, we are limited so it's difficult for us to realize, or at least admit, that some things are simply beyond us. We tend to measure things by our five senses, our mind, and a few years of history. However, God's got a much different method of measuring—Himself.

As noted in the references above, as well as a myriad of others, God is the only One who's really qualified to determine who, what, when, where, why, how much, how long or how far. Why? Because He's the only One who is <u>not</u> limited.

Only Elohim has a clear, unobstructed, unbiased, unhindered view of reality. Only El Shaddai has complete understanding of everything. Only El Roi sees the end from the beginning and everything in between. Only Jehovah Shammah is everywhere. Add all of God's other descriptive names to this list and it only makes the point more solid. Satan and all his powers of darkness nor humans nor anything else in creation can claim any of these things. Only God.

## CHAPTER 2

# The Challenge of Nearsightedness

It's human to stick with the familiar, due in great part to our limited way of grasping the bigger reality. For instance, most of us are familiar with that "someone" who will remain in a lifestyle or keep up a habit they clearly know is not good, but they're unwilling to change because at least it's familiar to them. Even though they're hurting, they fear the unknown world of change more than they fear the consequences of their present actions.

On the more positive side, even within Christian circles, we tend to go with what we're accustomed to. We know what we believe works scripturally, we've experienced God moving in certain ways over the years, we've heard countless testimonies, seen miracles with our own eyes and even had them happen to us. Consequently, over time we tend to assume these are the only ways God works.

The operative word here is "only." As people of the Word, we are certainly right to not vary from what's Scriptural, but since when does Scripture limit how God wants to work? Even though God will never contradict Himself, His everlasting Word leaves plenty of elbow room for God to do things His way, even if it has never been done before. As seen in the handful of verses in the previous chapter, God will do what God will do when and how He wants to do it.

Human nature is nearsighted and limited in thought. Even those who would be considered geniuses among us have miniscule brains when compared to God. This is not intended as a slam on the human race, but a reality check. As much of a miracle as we are in being created by God in His image (Genesis 1:27; Psalm 139:13-16) we come into this world damaged and very limited due to sin (thank you Adam and Eve). Seeing and living beyond our own personal experience and limitedness is something that doesn't come naturally to us. Thus, our only hope is to tap into the *super*-natural.

It is clear in God's Word He is not only a great big God but One who desires we move beyond where we currently are. This is reflected in the old adage, "God loves us just the way we are but loves us too much to leave us that way." As a general principle, I believe what is true for individuals is true for churches, ministries, and Christian organizations that God has raised up to impact His world. Why limit what God can do through us and in spite of us?

- For sinners, He wants us to move beyond our sin into salvation through faith in Jesus.

- For the saved, God desires we move beyond mere fire insurance to authentic discipleship.

- For disciples, God longs we move beyond simply doing the basics and into the realm of Spirit-filled living and power ministry as we make even more disciples.

- For churches and other ministries, God calls us to stretch ourselves beyond what we've previously accomplished and what we're used to, no matter how good, and onto a higher level of effectiveness to better meet the challenges of ministry in our present-day world.

In God, there's always a progression expected because He's bigger than we will ever completely know. There's more to following Him than what we have yet experienced, no matter how grand. As we already referenced, "His ways are higher than our ways," so it follows God can and will continue to reveal new and better ways to communicate His unchanging Word and disseminate His Spirit of power in order to accomplish His perfect plan.

In many ways, Scripture serves as God's telescope helping us "see" beyond where we are in the natural. Ephesians 3:20 is a view into the very heart of God and reveals with unmistakable clarity that He is a "beyond" God: "Now to Him who is able to do above and beyond all that we ask or think according to the power that works in us—". (HCSB)

Among other things, the terms "above" or "beyond" mean *over, superior to, exceeding abundantly, very highly, more.* In place of "think," some other translations use the word "imagine." These meanings and nuances are future-oriented, pertain to vision, nurture hope, spawn possibility thinking, necessitate that we stretch both our faith and expectations, are motivational, and speak of over-coming limitations both real and perceived.

> God can do anything you know—far more than you could ever imagine or guess or request in your wildest dreams! He does it not by pushing us around but by working within us, his Spirit deeply and gently within us.(Ephesians 3:20, 21 MSG)

Most of us are familiar with Buzz Lightyear, the famous animated co-star of the movie "A Toy Story." Even though I watched it with my grandkids (more than once!), I must say I loved this movie. We all remember the famous line Buzz triumphantly and courageously yells as he points to the sky, "To infinity and beyond!"

I'm not even sure this is possible because infinity is, well…never ending, and how can you get beyond something that's never ending? Anyway, if anyone can experience it or be there, it's God. My point is, any terminology related to the concept of "beyond" and all its facets is exciting, energizing and faith-building not to mention challenging and so very God-like! So, let's examine a few Scriptural examples of this and how we might practice this "beyond" mentality.

## CHAPTER 3

# An Abandoned Life

Oh, the depth of the riches and wisdom and knowledge of God! How unsearchable are his judgments and how fathomless his ways! For who has known the mind of the Lord, or who has been his counselor? Or who has first given to God, that God needs to repay him? For from him and through him and to him are all things. To him be glory forever! Amen. <u>Therefore</u>, I exhort you, brothers and sisters, by the mercies of God, to present your bodies as a sacrifice—alive, holy, and pleasing to God—which is your reasonable service. Do not be conformed to this present world, but be transformed by the renewing of your mind, so that you may test and approve what is the will of God—what is good and well-pleasing and perfect. (Romans 11:33-12:2 NET Bible, Underline is mine.)

It is not enough to simply trudge through life and/or ministry doing stuff we know to do simply because we know how to do it. Our call is much higher than mechanically going through the motions of ministry. Whether it be preaching, teaching, leading worship, writing, praying, visiting, you name it, God has not asked us to merely "do stuff". He's called and equipped us for world-changing life and ministry because He's a life-changing, miracle-working, world-changing God. In case some of us haven't noticed lately, God is quite big! Since God is so above and beyond us it is our call and duty to live life large by taking risks, much like a child would jump into the arms of a strong and trustworthy parent.

Romans 12:1 uses the transitional word "therefore." Basic English tells us it is the connecting link between what's gone before and comes after. Because of how God is described in the previous verses we can then do what's called for in the succeeding verses—live a sacrificial life and do His will.

Think of it this way, because the grandeur of God is so beyond us, we can certainly trust Him to guide and empower us to live the life and do the ministry He's asked of us. We can even go beyond what we thought we could do in scope, endurance and results. Recognizing God's ultimate control gives us confidence to not only live right, but to jump. The fullest expression of faith is seen in total abandonment in God.

When I was ordained, my pastor in Dallas gave me a large, parchment paper copy of a prayer John Wesley prayed annually on New Year's Day at the conclusion of his covenant service. The affect his life and ministry has had on world history is evidence Wesley clearly understood what abandonment means in view of our Beyond God.

> I am no longer by own, but thine. Put me to what thou wilt, rank me with whom thou wilt; put me to doing, put me to suffering; let me be employed for thee or laid aside for thee, exalted for thee or brought low for thee; let me be full, let me be empty; let me have all things, let me have nothing; I freely and heartily yield all things to thy pleasure and disposal.

> And now; O glorious and blessed God, Father, Son, and Holy Spirit, thou art mine, and I am thine. So be it. And the covenant which I have made on earth, let it be ratified in heaven. Amen.

## CHAPTER 4

# The Necessity of Endurance

We who consider ourselves "Spirit-filled" love to discuss, preach and teach about the gifts of the Spirit, miracles, the leading of God, and so much more that God does in, to and through us. These kinds of things usually get the majority of the press, and rightly so. However, there is a dimension of Spirit empowerment that is often overlooked in our discussions, much like David was left unnoticed in the shepherd's field when the search was on for a king. It is the concept of endurance.

Paul reports how the trustworthiness of our big God comes into play through trials we naturally encounter in life and as we pursue God's will.

> For we don't want you to be unaware, brothers, of our affliction that took place in Asia: we were completely overwhelmed—

beyond our strength—so that we even despaired of life. Indeed, we personally had a death sentence within ourselves, so that we would not trust in ourselves but in God who raises the dead. (II Corinthians 1:8-9)

Did he really say "beyond our strength"? How is that even possible short of death? It's because Paul and his companions had committed themselves to a God who lives and acts beyond earthly circumstances. They had learned to transfer their trust from their limited selves to their unlimited God who is the One really in control.

Anyone who plays sports, been in business, or served in the military knows that enduring through hard times is only par for the course of a true winner. This holds even more true for all Christians, especially those in ministry. I believe it's critical for us to place a much higher value on endurance than we may be in the habit of doing. Consider:

- What if Moses and the Israelites decided in the thirty-ninth year in the wilderness the journey was too hard and long so they went back to Egypt?

- What if David decided God's call for him was too tough and quit before he became king because Saul was determined to kill him? (I Samuel 18)

- What if Elisha had freaked out like his servant did when he saw they were surrounded by their enemy, stopping short of the miraculous victory God already had in mind? (II Kings 6)

- What if Daniel had given into impatience and gave up on day twenty of his twenty-one days of prayer and fasting before his answer arrived? (Daniel 10)

- What if Paul threw in the towel after he was, among other things, beaten and left for dead leaving a large portion of the New Testament unwritten? (II Corinthians 11:16ff)

- What if John decided that after he was abandoned to the Isle of Patmos (and tradition says also boiled in oil) he felt sorry for himself, surrendered to depression and refused to write Revelation?

- And, as long as we're at it, what if Jesus had given up? Where would the human race be then? (Hebrews 12:2)

As much as I hate to admit it, the church I pastor has had two major church problems that we in the church world call "splits," and they were only three years apart. The toll this takes on a pastor and his family is hard to describe. Thankfully, the last one happened nearly twenty years ago, but it's still not easy to talk about.

There were many factors that led to these, but during the last one I prayed a very short but extremely sincere prayer, "Lord, if You want me to leave this church and move on, we're certainly ready to go! But I have to know it's your will that we leave, otherwise we'll stay."

I must say I had to swallow hard praying that last phrase. During that time, I would get up to preach and as I looked out over the congregation I would think, "Lord, I know you called me to love these people, and I think I still do, but I don't like them very much right now."

To my comfort, I read where Moses had similar thoughts a time or two about the complaining congregation he led in the desert for 40 years. I was also reminded by my father-in-law that even God lost a third of his congregation when Lucifer and a number of angels decided to rebel.

Anyway, I was really, really, really hoping God would permit us to leave, but He didn't. We never felt the release. We were tired and worn out from stressful meetings, the rumor mill and the emotional roller coaster, so leaving appeared like the most favorable option. But our Beyond God wasn't through with us here. God performed some changes in us, we made some changes as a church, and nineteen years later we're still here, and the church is doing amazingly well as we close in on twenty-four years as pastor at Grace Christian Fellowship.

My wife, Pam, and I had been Christians long enough to know we shouldn't run just because there are problems. So, we endured the tough season and were finally able to actually see the sun and enjoy life and ministry again. I hazard to think where we might be if we would have cut and run from where we know God had called us to work His assignment. His grace is more than sufficient!

We must never underestimate the high value God places on endurance in fulfilling His plan and our call. Drawing from Bible characters and other mighty men and women of God throughout history, we can only conclude they were able to endure because they had a firm faith in a trustworthy God Who is above and beyond us all.

> And not only that, but we also rejoice in our afflictions, because we know that affliction produces endurance, endurance produces proven character, and proven character produces hope. This hope will not disappoint us, because God's love has been poured out in our hearts through the Holy Spirit who was given to us. (Romans 5:3-5)

Notice that the key to reaping the benefits of endurance is God's love poured generously into us by the Holy Spirit. The agape love of God is *the only* stabilizing factor in the middle of our tough times. If not for this fact every affliction would only drive us deeper into the ground of our dark circumstance. Instead, it is God's will that every challenging situation be viewed as an opportunity to fully trust God, stimulating our Godly character thereby releasing hope so it will raise us up beyond the present storm to win the day. Long sentence but a lot of truth. Boiled down, affliction becomes our friend in the hands of our Beyond God.

The times in which we live are getting increasingly tougher for bona fide Christians and those in the ministry. Thirty or forty years ago being a faithful Christian was seen by society as a big positive, something that was lauded. However, in the last several years we've seen a very deliberate cultural shift against Christians and the biblical values we hold dear. The liberal media and progressive elected officials are now attempting to cast faithful believers as hatemongers who are intolerant of others who need to be severely fined, or jailed, or both. In many parts of our nation, especially large cities with a higher concentration of secular, liberal thought, practicing genuine Christianity in the marketplace has become taboo. For instance:

- Who would have thought we'd see the day that politely refusing to bake a cake for a lesbian "wedding" on the grounds of faith conviction would be worthy of a lawsuit? Such is the plight of Aaron and Melissa Klein who were found guilty of discrimination and ordered to pay $135,000 costing them their business and future investment for their children.

- Who could have seen the day when a Christian photographer, Elaine Huguenin, who runs Elane Photography in New Mexico and kindly refused to take pictures for a gay ceremony in 2006 because it went against her beliefs, would have been found guilty of discrimination? One New Mexico Supreme Court Justice even went so far as to say that surrendering their freedom is "the price of citizenship." Indeed.

- A few years ago, we would never have thought it possible that an older Christian couple would have faced a multi-thousand-dollar lawsuit because they graciously said that a farm they transformed into a place for weddings could not be used for a gay ceremony.

- Many of us have heard about Barronelle Stutzman, the owner of Arlene's Flowers in Richland, Washington. Even though she has served and even employed homosexuals for years, the American Civil Liberties Union and the Washington attorney general have charged her with unlawful discrimination because she politely refused to do flower arrangements for a male friend's same-sex ceremony. The case is currently headed to the U.S. Supreme Court.

Having a pit-bull attitude is essential and priceless to God as we tenaciously hold onto our biblical convictions and God's call. Without it, fulfilling our destiny is nearly, if not entirely, impossible. We know this to be true because God spells "success"—f-a-i-t-h-f-u-l.

Endurance. Don't leave home without it.

## CHAPTER 5

# Beyond Our Self

There's a saying that's been around in various forms for many years: "When you find yourself where God is all you have, you realize He's all you need." This isn't some fairy-tale saying, it's biblical.

A person can't read long in the Bible before we run into someone who has an assignment from God but find they're at the end of their "self". Because we serve a Beyond God, we could say it this way, "You can do more than you think you can."

Moses didn't have great credentials. In fact, if ever there was a basket case it was Moses! (Pun intended.) We know the story. He was hidden by his mother to save his life, was found by Pharaoh's daughter who wanted to spare him then hired Moses' mother to take care of him until he was old enough to be raised by Pharaoh's daughter herself.

Even though Moses was raised in the king's palace his heart remained true to God's people. God saw this passion in Moses and called him to lead His people out of Egypt to the Promised Land. And what was Moses' response to God's call? "Get someone else!" Thankfully, God continued to pursue him until Moses reluctantly relented. History records a former murderer called Moses, became one of the greatest leaders of all time.

Moses couldn't conceive that he was capable of doing what God was asking. Our Beyond God was, indeed, requesting Moses to do a job that was bigger than him, much bigger, and Moses knew it.

More often than not, the vision of ministry God plants in us is bigger than us. Some would say it's always bigger than us or it's probably not from God, and I would not disagree. So, the question really isn't about the size of the vision, our limitations or lack of resources, but rather the size of our Beyond God. Moses discovered, with God as his protector and provider, that he could do more than he thought he could. His Beyond God helped him get beyond himself.

Are you standing in your way? Are you limiting what God might desire to do through you because you're convinced you're not qualified? So often we manage to create a smoke-screen we hide behind made up of fears and false information about who we are or what we're unable to do in order to rationalize why we haven't accomplished more. This all-too-common condition makes it difficult to see beyond the "limitation haze."

As a brief side note, I'm not saying God doesn't have certain timetables within which His will functions. After all, He does have a plan and plans have timetables which usually include training, testing and spiritual growth (think forty years in the wilderness). I'm also not advocating we simply run around driven by mere zealousness, which only results in frustrating God's plan for us, not to mention driving people crazy.

What I am saying is we are often our own worst enemy when it comes to moving forward in accomplishing God's assignment for us. Unless and until we learn how to look beyond ourselves, we will not be able to realize God's ability to work through us in ways we think are impossible.

When I was younger I took swimming lessons at a local lake near where I lived. It was fun, and at the age of seven my only desire was to, well, play. Everyone started in the beginner class and, if a person followed the instructions, at some point you could take a swimming test. If you passed, they would move you up to the next level.

I loved playing in the shallow water of the beginner class. It was all about me having fun. I didn't pay much attention to the teacher, in fact two years later I was still in the beginner class, piddling in the puddles.

One day I found myself being bored and as I looked around I realized I was not only the tallest kid in the class but all my friends were in higher levels than me. I decided I would take the test. I passed. I went to the next level and after few minutes I asked the teacher if I could take the test. I passed. The same thing happened the next three levels. Before I knew it, I had advanced from the lowest level to the highest in less than 30 minutes. Look out Michael Phelps!

The point is, we can usually do more than we have allowed ourselves. God doesn't limit us, we do. The teachers in my swimming classes weren't limiting me, I was limiting myself by focusing only on myself. Once I began to realize my potential I gained confidence and moved beyond where I was to levels I never dreamed of.

I have often said from the pulpit, "Jesus died on the cross for our sins and our excuses." Sure, we're human. Of course, we are not God. It goes without saying, left to our devices we have the uncanny ability to mess things up, and quite well, I might add. However, God specializes in using imperfect, limited humans.

Following God's call is not about you or me or "them", it's about taking God at His Word, being filled with Holy Spirit power—"Christ in you the hope of glory"—then moving forward with that confidence. And when we do, accomplishing the Great Commission becomes more than a quaint Sunday School lesson.

## CHAPTER 6

# So, What About Maturity?

For this very reason, make every effort to add
to your faith... (II Peter 1:5)

When the topic of spiritual growth comes up
it's interesting to hear how various people
define it. Some measure growth by the number
of years a person has been a professing Christian.
Others would gage it by a significant knowledge of
the Bible and having a myriad of verses memorized.
Another person might evaluate the level of maturity
by the frequency of signs, wonders and miracles in
someone's everyday life or ministry. Yet someone else
may understand spiritual growth is evidenced when
a person has a greatly reduced "sin rate".

While these can and often do serve as indicators of a person's progression as a follower of Jesus they also may not always be reliable for various reasons. At this point we must be extremely careful because outside of evaluating a person, including our self, by our "fruit" (whatever that means) our ability to measure someone else can quickly cross over to judgement, which we know is God's gig alone.

This said, the Bible is clear God not only desires us to mature but requires it if we are to have any significant degree of effectiveness in the world. This is why we must rely on Scripture to help us know what authentic Christian maturity looks like. As we shall see, God's heart is that we certainly move beyond where we currently are to a higher plane of life with Him, whatever this looks like.

As a pastor for many years I've seen things in people that rightly cause us to question how far a person has actually grown, if at all. How well we know that when a person gets "saved" this does not mean all problems automatically disappear. How we wish this were so. While the wrestling match with our human nature continues in many ways, we have a most excellent Coach who not only loves us but has declared each of us a winner. As such, He will use various ways and means to motivate and equip us so we move forward to be strong in life and successful in ministry.

A premier Scripture highlighting God's desire we move beyond our current level is II Peter 1:3-11. He first references the provision of our Beyond God.

> His divine power has given us everything required for life and godliness through the knowledge of Him who called us by His own glory and goodness. By these He has given us very great and precious promises, so that through them you may share in the divine nature, escaping the corruption that is in the world because of evil desires. (VV.3, 4 HCSB)

It's important to note this truth is available to and expected of everyone. It's not just for select persons or groups, for God is an equal opportunity Coach. Secondly, He gives something only a Coach like He can give, divine power!

A good coach is not satisfied with us simply showing up for the game (think life) but that we would work at improving our own ability so we can contribute to the team's efforts (advancing the kingdom) in ever-increasing ways. It's His job to train and equip us, and it's our job to listen, learn, know the playbook (Scripture), and give our best effort on the field (ministry) and off (personal life). If we do, we'll get better; if we don't, we won't.

A main principle throughout God's Word is that our relationship with God is a combination of God's provision and our effort. We are not robots nor are we slaves. We are God's Spirit-empowered sons and daughters. To move beyond where we are in both private life and public ministry requires both.

This partnership principal is active in II Peter 1 in the various aspects of growth as we move beyond our human limitations.

FAITH – The beginning point and foundation on which the other aspects rest as we take God at His Word, trusting Him fully.

GOODNESS – Can be defined as the excellence and courage in the art of living well. It occurs as we live out the goodness of Jesus already in us.

KNOWLEDGE – Comes from the Greek word "gnosis" and it's relative "sophia," which is wisdom defined as "knowledge of things both human and divine, and of their causes". Together they mean practical knowledge of how to apply wisdom.

SELF-CONTROL – Refers to "self-mastery, the ability to take a grip on oneself." Because this is also listed in the "fruit of the Spirit" in Galatians 5, this tells us we are able to enjoy yet control our earthly passions because of God's Spirit inside us.

PERSEVERANCE – This stems from a Greek word meaning "the voluntary and daily suffering of hard and difficult things for the sake of honor and usefulness."
Godly perseverance always has a forward look as we courageously accept everything

life can do to us and using it as yet another step on the upward way.

GODLINESS – This indicates we have a right relationship with both God and other people. We worship and serve God passionately as well as respecting and serving others. It exhibits the heart of a self-sacrificing servant.

BROTHERLY KINDNESS – Comes from the word "philadelphia" meaning "love of the brethren." We are to demonstrate kindness to everyone, but especially to other believers. For example, when someone falls into sin, rather than condemning, brotherly kindness says we minister healing and restoration to them.

LOVE – "Agape", refers to the unconditional, unstoppable, ever-widening love of God. Since the source is our Heavenly Father it must flow from Him through us. This is the common thread running through all the other characteristics providing us with proper motivation and application.

Taken together, these help elevate us beyond temporal, selfish activity and mere human reaction to the place of Christlikeness. There are two important things to remember here: 1) It's a partnership between God and each of us individually and, 2) There will always be a need for growth in each of these while on this earth.

Peter highlights the value of this in verse 8: "For as these qualities are yours and are increasing [in you as you grow toward spiritual maturity], they will keep you from being useless and unproductive in regard to the true knowledge and greater understanding of our Lord Jesus Christ." (AMP)

As seen throughout the Bible, this "true knowledge and greater understanding" leads to our increased usefulness to God and productivity in eternal things as we participate in God's divine nature and eternal plan.

## Chapter 7

# Beyond Discontent

One of the dangers of examining the nature of "beyondness" is to become discontent with where we are in life or ministry. If we're not careful we will wake up every day anxious to get "beyond" wherever it is we think we are. Some have even said we should have a holy discontent with where we are so we don't become complacent and miss the next stage of life or ministry God has for us.

While I obviously agree with this in general, thus the theme of this book, I believe there's nothing "holy" about fleshly discontentment. I don't believe for an instant we are called to walk around every day feeling anxious, constantly worrying we aren't doing enough or afraid we missed God or circumstances aren't what we need them to be or we don't have enough money to proceed with what we feel God has called us to do, and on and on it goes.

I am very familiar with this feeling, as I know most (all?) pastors are. We become pastor of a church and we're all enthusiastic. We have big dreams and make exciting plans, some from God, some not (as we eventually realize). We soon discover a few of our people aren't nearly as excited about the vision of our church as we are. A negative atmosphere begins to develop. As time passes growth is slower than we want, finances needed are more than we imagined, attendance drops and some grumbling begins. (I think I hear Moses saying, "I can relate!"). A spirit infiltrates the church and it's anything but holy.

When discontentment begins to raise its ugly head, the focus slowly shifts from passionately following God's vision to frantically putting out fires. This is hard on a guy who wrestles with people-pleasing. My family and I discovered the hard way there is nothing anyone can do to please some people. Add to this a circumstance that emerges we hadn't foreseen nor wanted and you have a recipe for discontentment, or worse, its bigger, uglier brother, discouragement.

The above is just one example among many of how discontentment can envelope a person or a ministry. Sometimes it develops from very personal things like a poor self-image or past failures. Other times it can creep up on you as you get battle weary or just plain weary with the number of responsibilities required of us on a daily basis. In many ways, discontentment can enter via the cultural atmosphere in a community, or even a nation. Satan often uses this to stifle churches and cause disunity in a geographic area. Studies in spiritual warfare bear this out. After a while simply maintaining the status quo seems very inviting, but is also the place where discontentment grows deep roots.

The possibility to be discontented is always a temptation. The Apostle Paul had to deal with it. In fact, knowing the many challenges he faced I am quite sure it was a regular struggle for him. (See I Corinthians 16:8-9 and II Corinthians 11:16-33 for examples).

In Philippians, he explains how he learned to overcome discontentment. I will use the Amplified version because it paints the picture so clearly how he grew beyond allowing discontentment to hinder him.

> Not that I speak from [any personal] need, for I have learned to be content [and self-sufficient through Christ, satisfied to the point where I am not disturbed or uneasy] regardless of my circumstances. I know how to get along and live humbly [in difficult times], and I also know how to enjoy abundance and live in prosperity. In any and every circumstance I have learned the secret [of facing life], whether well-fed or going hungry, whether having an abundance

or being in need. I can do all things [which He has called me to do] through Him who strengthens and empowers me [to fulfill His purpose—I am self-sufficient in Christ's sufficiency; I am ready for anything and equal to anything through Him who infuses me with inner strength and confident peace.] (Philippians 4:11-13 AMP)

The following are two modern-day portraits of Godly contentment.

### Portrait #1...

I recently attended an Upward basketball game one of my grandsons played in. Upward is a nation-wide, Christian-based sports program for children. At halftime, the director of the program gave a brief message on Philippians 4:13. He related that one time as he was refereeing he noticed a guy on one of the teams had "Phil. 4:13" written on the bottom of his shoes. A few minutes later he noticed that same verse written on the shoes of a player on the opposing team. He asked himself, "If I were God how would I answer those prayers they both prayed to win?"

That got him to thinking about the meaning of this verse. He knew both teams consisted of mostly Christian boys and both teams were praying that they would win and both teams sincerely believed that the way to win was to trust that Jesus would give them the ability to beat the socks off the other team.

The director finished by emphasizing that because of the verses that go before regarding being content whatever the circumstance, Philippians 4:13 has nothing to do with winning some physical sport. It has everything to do with looking beyond the earthly challenges by fixing our eyes on heavenly things—the things that really count.

In this life, we sometimes experience loss but God always defines victory in spiritual terms and Christlike attitude, thus the real rewards are often delayed or even come veiled in apparent failure. Paul was able to "boast in the Lord" because his Beyond God did great things through him in spite of his weakness (II Corinthians 11:30).

### Portrait #2...

James Strickland introduced himself to me after a Wednesday night service at my church. He said he had moved to Poplar Bluff recently and was looking for a home church. In the course of his introduction he said he was a felon and had been released from prison only two years before. When I asked him how long of a sentence he had served he replied, "Oh, about 49 years."

It's important to understand our church is somewhat used to felons attending as we are in close partnership with an addiction recovery ministry. Most of these, however, have served much less time behind bars, indeed some several times, but even then, none came close to James' record.

In one of our small group meetings James shared his testimony of how he was first incarcerated in 1968, then was in and out of prison several times before he was finally convicted of murder. He escaped twice but was soon caught which only increased his sentence.

Along the way, someone gave him a Bible and he began to read about some men and women with bad records that God used powerfully. James related to Moses the murderer, David the adulterer/murderer, Jacob the deceiver, Rahab the prostitute, Peter the denier, Paul the persecutor and many others. It began to dawn on him that if God could use them then maybe there was hope for him, too.

As it happened, at about the same time an FBI agent, who had tracked him down and arrested him, was a committed Christian and began visiting James on his own free time. He simply witnessed to him about the love of Jesus. Then it happened. In 1982 James Strickland surrendered again, but this time wholeheartedly to Jesus Christ while in prison.

A holy glow grew to an amazing blaze and it wasn't long before James found himself witnessing to the other inmates. In each prison he rotated to, James ministered in any way he could. He eventually felt God leading him to begin a Christian newsletter that was circulated among the other inmates. He also wrote other material introducing prisoners to Jesus Christ in addition to encouraging and strengthening fellow believers. His reputation for being relentless in sharing Christ, added to fearlessness in who he shared with and coupled with his positive attitude, provided James with special favor in the eyes of wardens.

Because of the seriousness of his charges he had settled into the idea he would spend the rest of his natural life incarcerated, which is why no one was more surprised than James when he was released due to no action of his own. It was nothing short of a miracle. He was set free on the outside 32 years after being set free on the inside.

It goes without saying James Strickland had many opportunities to become discontent. Rather, he chose contentment in Christ and ministry to others "whatever the circumstance". His Beyond Lord had an irrevocable call on his life and nothing would stop Him from fulfilling it. Indeed, he became a modern-day Paul, literally singing with his guitar and preaching to the prisoners every week. However, because many of his fellow, unsaved inmates felt very uncomfortable in the chapel, James was allowed to hold church in another location. Only heaven will reveal how many he has led to Jesus and encouraged in the faith, especially in the sanctuary under the tree outside the gas chamber.

## CHAPTER 8

# Power for Purity

Beyond all question, the mystery of godliness is great: He appeared in a body, was vindicated by the Spirit, was seen by angels, was preached among the nations, was believed on in the world, was taken up in glory. (I Timothy 3:16)

Even though our Beyond God has equipped us for "everything we need for life and godliness" (II Peter 1:3) many Christians struggle with personal purity. Most of us know that pornography is more rampant now than ever in history, thanks to modern technology. It's also becoming more known the problem is not limited to those "in the world," but is also a struggle with many who identify as born-again Christians, even those in ministry.

In a recent survey/study commissioned by Josh McDowell Ministries and conducted by Barna Research it was discovered 21% of youth pastors and 14% of pastors admitted they currently struggled with porn to some degree. This is shocking, but when combined with the numbers of the general Christian population, which are even worse, it becomes obvious we have a many-tentacled monster on our hands that requires something beyond us to defeat. *("The Porn Phenomenon", by the Barna Group, (https://www.barna.org) and Josh McDowell Ministry (https://www.josh.org).*

Obviously, there are numerous moral issues in addition to pornography that are lurking around every corner. Rampant drug addiction, dishonesty in government, greed, materialism, racism, TV, movies and video games laced with sexual and violent themes, are just a few of other types of "tentacles".

Anyone who has ever wrestled with drug addiction and is honest, will tell you they could never have overcome it by themselves. The church I pastor is closely connected with "Crossroads", a ministry to those with addiction. We have seen many addicts not only attend our worship services, but go to the Sunday afternoon service Crossroads holds at a neutral location for those who don't feel accepted in the normal church setting (which should tell us something…). It is always exciting when we see someone who is desperate for freedom surrender to Jesus Christ as their only hope. I have to say that few things are more powerful than a fired-up former addict!

Crossroads Ministry is noted for their victory cry as they always shout the name, "JESUS!", often at random times. His name is shouted at the close of every worship service we have at my church as well as Crossroads worship and other times. As most born-again addicts will tell you, if it wasn't for the unconditional love and unlimited power of Jesus they would never have gotten outside the grip of their addiction. Their Beyond God set them free in a way they never knew was possible.

As good and helpful as 12-step programs can be, Crossroads has a much simpler version that meets on Tuesday evenings in our fellowship hall. Its official name is "Won by One," the shortened form being "One Step," referring to the most important step in any person's life—full submission to Jesus Christ. As addiction's realities are discussed, it is emphasized over and over again that only by the power of Jesus—the Living Word, and Scripture—the written Word, can true and lasting deliverance come. They know first-hand what it means to have Jehovah Rophe show up and personally present them with something "above and beyond all they could ask or imagine."

## CHAPTER 9

# Chasing Lions

One Tuesday night following jail ministry, I was standing around talking to one of the inmates. He told me about a book that had opened his eyes to his own potential as seen through the eyes of our big God. It was a book with a strange title, kind of long actually, yet intriguing: *In a Pit with a Lion on a Snowy Day – How to Survive and Thrive When Opportunity Roars*, by Mark Batterson. (© 2006 by Mark Batterson, Multnomah Publishers, 2016 revised edition).

I had heard of the book but didn't have the interest to read it until then. The next day I ordered it and read it on vacation. As I read it, I became increasingly excited and just a little disappointed; excited about the potential we all have but disappointed I hadn't taken advantage of it.

The book is based on a relatively obscure passage of Scripture concerning some feats of Benaiah, especially when he chased down and killed a lion…

> Benaiah son of Jehoiada, a valiant fighter from Kabzeel, performed great exploits. He struck down Moab's two mightiest warriors. He also went down into a pit on a snowy day and killed a lion. And he struck down a huge Egyptian. Although the Egyptian had a spear in his hand, Benaiah went against him with a club. He snatched the spear from the Egyptian's hand and killed him with his own spear. (II Samuel 23:20-21)

The objective here is not to preach this passage or quote large segments from Batterson's book but to make the point that you and I serve the same Beyond God that Benaiah did. The book points out that because Benaiah had a careless kind of faith in a great big God he knew he could take risks. Not risks for risk sake, but for God's sake and that of others. Benaiah eventually became David's main man in charge of his bodyguard before becoming commander-in-chief of Israel's army.

To quote Batterson,

> There is an old aphorism: 'No guts, no glory.' When we don't have the guts to step out on faith and chase lions, then God is robbed of the glory that rightfully belongs to him… Maybe we've measured spiritual maturity the wrong way. Maybe following Christ isn't

as safe or as civilized as we've been led to believe. Maybe Christ was more dangerous and uncivilized than our Sunday-school flannelgraphs portrayed. Maybe God is raising up a generation of lion chasers." (pp. 19-20)

My point is this, if we really are convinced we serve a God who is willing to go "above and beyond all we ask or imagine," isn't this kind of God worth our wholehearted commitment?

## CHAPTER 10

# Beyond the Box

Q: What human being has experienced all of God that exists and all the ways He works?
A: No one!

If there's one thing I've learned it's that God will do things His way in his time using whoever and whatever He wants. After all, He is the God of infinite variety—people, animals, bugs, sea life, snowflakes, you name it. In my imagination, I often visualize God gently jabbing one of the angels in the side as they peer over the portal of heaven and, with a slight smile on His face, God remarks, "Watch how I do this one!"

Look, I am about to do something new; even now it is coming. Do you not see it?

Indeed, I will make a way in the wilderness, rivers in the desert. (Isaiah 43:19 HCSB)

Consider a small sampling of the variety of methods God uses in accomplishing His purposeful plan:

- Enoch walked faithfully with God; then "God took him away." (Genesis 5:24)

- Noah heard the voice of God tell him to build a great big boat because He was going to destroy the world with a flood, whatever *that* was. (Genesis 6:14-18)

- I can only imagine what those conversations with God felt like as Abraham heard God tell him to pack up, pick up then go to an unknown land. (Genesis 12:1)

- Along comes Moses who witnesses God get Pharaoh's attention with several nation-wide plagues before leading the children of Israel into the desert while He provided a couple million people with all their needs and performing numerous miracles for forty years. Whew! (Exodus 7-40; Deuteronomy)

- Water flows from a rock. (Numbers 20:7-11)

- A donkey talks. (Numbers 22:28-30)

- David kills a lion, a bear and a 9-foot giant before he reaches driving age (chariots…?) prior to going on to become one of the greatest kings in history. (I Samuel 17:34-50; II Samuel 5:1-4, 8:1-6)

- A flock of ugly black birds feeds a prophet. (I Kings 17:5, 6)

- An iron axe head floats. (II Kings 6:5-7)

- A fish becomes the first ATM. (Matthew 17:27)

- A nameless blind man receives his sight by mud being placed on his eyes made from the spit of Jesus. (John 9:6, 7)

- A dead man hears the life-giving voice of Jesus call his name and comes back to life. And I imagine Lazarus had a much easier time than most believing in the resurrection of Jesus! (John 11:43, 44)

- Stephen saw the very face of Christ as his earthly life slipped away making him the first martyr in the New Testament. (Acts 7:54-60)

- Paul, blinded by a brilliant light, heard the audible voice of Jesus and answered the call to ministry risking his life to do so. (Acts 9:3-19)

I would guess most of us don't need to be convinced of the unfathomable power of God, but I would venture to say we might need reminding of the variety of ways God uses to display it. We see in Scripture the truth that while God Himself never changes, his methods often do. Since He is Creator God He can do a "new thing" at any time, and I suspect He might do so at times just because He can and so we will keep our eyes on Him. Methods aren't meant to be worshipped, only God is.

I can't recall exactly where I read this but recently I came across a story that demonstrates both the power of prayer and God working beyond the "box" of our expectations.

A woman in a predominately Muslim country heard the gospel and became born-again through faith in Jesus Christ. Of course, this meant she now lived in high risk because her husband was a very committed Muslim. For many weeks, the only place this woman could pray and worship her Savior was in the bathroom of her home, and she did so faithfully. As you can imagine, one of her main prayers was that her husband would come to know Jesus.

The husband eventually discovered she had become a Christian and got extremely upset. A few days went by with the woman in constant anticipation of her eminent death by her husband as an "honor killing," something she was willing to endure for the love of Jesus.

One day the husband decided it was time to do it, but on the way to kill his wife he got into a very serious accident. As it happened, the only hospital within many miles was run by Christians so he was taken there. Severely injured with life-threatening injuries, the Muslim man was rolled into the operating room and put to sleep for surgery.

While under anesthesia the man had an encounter with Jesus. As earthly doctors were working on his body God was working on his soul. The man fully surrendered to Jesus while his body was still fully sedated.

After he awoke the man couldn't wait to tell of his experience with Jesus, that he had become a

Christian. After the initial shock of those who heard him, especially his wife, they all cried tears of joy and praised Jesus for this very unusual (to us) method of intervening in this man's life. A man who was put to sleep a Muslim killer, woke up a Christian believer!

After the poke in the ribs and the miracle occurs, I imagine God smiling and saying to his angels, "I love doing this stuff!"

## Chapter 11

# God's Mighty Muscle

According to the power that works in us.
(Ephesians 3:20b)

What we've really been discussing all along is some of the ways and means of how the unlimited power of God works. After all, the call and command from God is for us to walk daily in the power of His Holy Spirit (i.e. John 14:17; 16:13-15; Acts 1:8; Romans 8:5-11; Galatians 5:16, 25; Ephesians 5:18, etc.). None of what we have previously discussed is possible without the very Spirit of God Himself inside us, beside us, in front of us, behind us, above us, beneath us and at work in the world around us.

On the day of Pentecost (Acts 2), the Holy Spirit came as a "mighty, rushing wind" and "tongues of fire" resulting in one hundred and twenty people being filled with indescribable power, speaking in unknown languages, and finally ending the day with over three thousand souls being saved. Quite a grand entrance into this world, wouldn't you say? It's not that the Holy Spirit wasn't active before then, but from that day on, individuals functioning as the church, the Body of Christ, were empowered to do a work that would literally change the course of history in a brand new "surge" of power.

Yet, in spite of all this, many people still do not have a clear idea who the Holy Spirit really is and His purpose in our call to Christlikeness.

In his gospel, John uses the Greek term "parakletos" in reference to the Holy Spirit. It can be translated into English as *counselor, helper, encourager, advocate,* or *comforter.* However, the most common description is "one who stands by to help," or "one called alongside to help."

The Holy Spirit is not an "it", or a mere emotional feeling that gives us warm fuzzies when we're around other Christians, like rabid fans at some sporting event, or even some nebulous force "out there" somewhere.

The Holy Spirit is a <u>person</u>, with the same power and authority as God the Father and Jesus Christ the Son. In His teaching in John 14:15-20 Jesus referred to the Holy Spirit as comforter or counselor or advocate or helper (depending on the translation) and was, in fact, referring to Himself (V. 18). Verse 20 goes even further, painting the picture still more vividly of how the entire trinity is intimately involved with us: "In that day you will know that I am in my father, you are in me, and I am in you."

Without the activity of the Holy Spirit there is no salvation, we cannot know the truth, the church could not exist, we have no power and the advancement of the gospel ceases. Even though the Holy Spirit has been around and active since before day one (Genesis 1:2), the day of Pentecost introduced us to a new expression of God. He knew we needed an additional infusion of power in these last days to help us get the job done of making disciples of all nations, so in His sovereign plan He poured out His power like never before in history.

While it is a fact the Holy Spirit comes into us when we repent and receive Jesus Christ as our Savior thus creating the miracle of being born-again, Jesus, the book of Acts, and most of Paul's writings among other Scriptures, confirm there is more power available. Jesus told His disciples a greater ability would be given them so that they could be effective in changing the world for Him. We need incredible ability to do the things God has called us to do and He's not going to request something and not equip us for the task!

Imagine, God wants to use us in spite of us—in spite of our past sin, limitations, mistakes and imperfections—to win the lost and disciple the saved. Acts 1:8 declares we are God's "Plan A" and He has no "Plan B." As far as God's concerned, we're it. Yet He's well aware we need a power beyond our own to complete the assignment.

I remember the story of Lock Benali, a young boy from Nepal, who gave his life to Christ. His own father had him arrested and was sentenced 4-6 years for sharing Jesus with everyone. He was put in jail with eighteen hardened criminals. He won them all to Christ! The authorities finally kicked him out of jail nine months later because he was too much trouble!

The law in Nepal said he couldn't be prosecuted for the same crime twice. Lock began a regular preaching ministry and is now the pastor of a church of several thousand. Lock's love for Jesus combined with the power of Holy Spirit worked like nitroglycerine helping him accomplish something that was well beyond his ability alone.

Many years ago, I read about a ministry trip Loren Cunningham, who worked with YWAM (Youth With A Mission), made to Tonga.

> During an open-air meeting, one of our workers placed her purse on the ground. The next minute it disappeared. The thief who ran off with it must have been disappointed—there was no money or credit cards, only a bunch of Tongan gospel tracts!

He tossed the purse over the palace wall. The young prince found it and passed the literature out to the king's household. Later, many in the palace came to know Jesus, too.

In the following weeks, our teams visited every village of the island nation. They preached in houses, churches, and in various schools. At one girl's school, almost every student gave her life to Jesus.

While teaching worship choruses, Kalafi felt led to stand up and command them, 'Receive the Holy Ghost!' Although the girls had never had such teaching, and no other explanation was given, they were all simultaneously filled with the Spirit and began loudly praying in tongues! Several stood on chairs to give prophecies—something else they had never been taught to do. (Ministries Today, May/June 1994)

You can't tell me some angels didn't have some sore ribs by the end of that trip! (Give it time, it'll come to you...)

## CHAPTER 12

# Wrestling with Sovereignty

It would be safe to assume there is probably no other aspect of God that is harder for most of us to grasp than God's sovereignty. While we may say we believe and trust God in all circumstances, it's much harder to actually do this when things don't go as we expected, desired, or believed. However, if we fail to come to a reasonable understanding of God's sovereignty we will be in a constant state of frustration and struggle in our faith.

In numerous places Scripture declares this crucial view of God:

The Lord reigns for ever and ever. (Exodus 15:18)

...for dominion belongs to the Lord and He rules over the nations. (Psalm 22:28)

Our God is in heaven; He does whatever pleases him. (Psalm 115:3)

In his discourse on eating food offered to idols Paul takes the opportunity to delve into the nature of God's sovereignty, "...yet for us there is but one God, the Father, from whom all things came and for whom we live; and there is but one Lord, Jesus Christ, through whom all things came and through whom we live" (I Corinthians 8:6).

And then there's Job, whose understanding is probably clearer than almost anyone else, hopefully for obvious reasons. Chapter nine deals with God's sovereignty from many angles but he seems to sum it up in verse 12, "If He snatches away, who can stop Him? Who can say to Him, 'what are you doing?'"

The best and simplest definition of sovereignty is this: God is in control of everything. And this is exactly where we humans have our problem. Whether it's human pride wanting to have complete control over our own lives, or we believe we know what God's specific will is in a given situation, or we are hurting so much we hope beyond hope God will do things a certain way in order for us to have some relief from the pain, it's a big pill to swallow.

I like how J. I. Packer puts it:

> Divine Sovereignty is a vast subject: it embraces everything that comes into the biblical picture of God as Lord and King in this world, the one who 'worketh all things

after the counsel of his own will' (Ephesians 1:11), directing every process and ordering every event for the fulfilling of his own eternal plan. (Packer, J. I., *Evangelism and the Sovereignty of God*, as quoted in www. allaboutgod.com.)

So where does all of this leave us as we get our minds and hearts around our Beyond God? I believe it's ultimately about childlike faith. When we were children we sincerely believed our mom or dad could do no wrong. Mom was the best cook, greatest comforter and most gifted doctor as she knew just how to put that band aid on our scratched knee and dry our tears. Dad was the strongest, bravest being on the planet, almost god-like. This led to the sincere belief that he could make or fix anything or, better yet, "My daddy can beat up your daddy!" we would yell as we climbed the monkey bars.

It has always fascinated me that God has, at the same time, called us to both Christlikeness and childlikeness. Christlikeness causes us to live like Jesus in every area of life while childlikeness results in trusting God the Father in every situation whether we understand or not…especially not! We can only have confidence in God with the unpredictables of life if we have a firm belief in His powerful love and simple faith He knows what He's doing in and through the realities of life.

While this subject deserves much more discussion, it does bring us to an inevitable topic crucial to surviving and thriving within the frequent unpredict-ability of our present world. Truth is, it's at the heart of being able to flow with God's sovereign nature.

## CHAPTER 13

# Trust – a Beyond Thing

March 4, 2009 will forever be etched into our souls as the day the lives of our family got turned upside down. We received a phone call that our 29-year-old daughter, Stephanie, had suddenly collapsed in her home. Because attempts at reviving her failed this moment in time became her graduation to heaven. Up to this point she had been perfectly healthy, happily married to a Christian man, two young children, and very active in her home church. This made absolutely no sense to us, and still doesn't.

The outpouring of love we received from relatives, friends past and present, our own church family, and people we didn't even know, was evidence of the many lives she touched during her abbreviated stint here on earth. It was, and still is, a somewhat surreal event, like watching a tragic movie about someone else's life. Only if a person has been through something similar can they relate to the questions and roller coaster of emotions.

However, let it never be said we got angry at God or blamed Him in any way. I know many people who find themselves in similar situations do, and understandably so, but this is not our story. Even though our minds didn't understand and we had (and still have) many questions, our faith encouraged us to trust God, so we did.

There were three major truths God showed us through this, and all have to do with trusting God beyond worldly circumstances.

First, when the gale-force winds of circumstance were blowing all around us our God was our anchor like never before. We prayed over and over again, "I trust you, Lord! I trust you, Lord! I trust you, Lord!" We were holding onto Him for dear life and, to be perfectly honest, our sanity. The power of positive, Biblically-based confession had never been as powerful in its ability to walk us through those heart-wrenching days of grief.

Second, worship of our trust-worthy God became our healing balm. For my wife, Pam, this became very personal. She has shared many times that the peace of God would return to her troubled mind when she worshipped because in that atmosphere our soul gets its focus back on our loving

God. In addition, knowing Stephanie was now in a worship-filled atmosphere in heaven 24/7 brought consolation in the possibility that, in the midst of our praise, we were closer to her also as we visualized her doing the same thing.

Third, God revealed an understanding of authentic faith beyond what we understood it to be up to that point. Following the funeral, we stayed two weeks to help with the grandkids. On the ten-hour drive home I was praying about what I would say to the people at the church I pastored, many of whom had made the long trip to Texas to be with us.

My immediate family, along with a few close friends, had prayed for a resurrection. We all were strongly confident it would happen by actually praying for her prior to her being embalmed and fully believing the Scripture that "with God, all things are possible" (Matthew 19:16; Mark 10:27, etc.).

The resurrection didn't occur. But strangely enough, we left that small, drab room at the funeral home that day with a "peace that passes all understanding", knowing we had done everything we could do, spiritually speaking. As a declaration of faith, I remarked as we were walking out, "I believe Stephanie can be resurrected until we put her in the ground."

My dilemma was, given that the miracle didn't happen; what is the best thing I could say as a pastor to my congregation that would be authentic in light of the circumstance yet faithful to God at the same time?

On a boring stretch of Highway 67 north of Little Rock, Arkansas God said, "Tell them faith is not always measured by outward results, but by obedience to my Word." Tears welled as it dawned on me that faith had a facet I had not considered until now.

We often refer to the Scripture that declares that "signs and wonders will follow those who believe" (i.e. Mark 16:17). While we undoubtedly believe this to be true, what do we do with the elephant in the room that suddenly appears when we have great faith, pray diligently and see no outward results? How should we respond when the healing doesn't come, finances fall short, our loved one doesn't get saved, or in our case, our desired miracle of a resurrected daughter does not happen?

Our Beyond God seems to be saying, "If you invest your faith fully in me and commit to being a doer of My Word, then you get credit in your heavenly bank account regardless of what you don't see." When acting in bold faith from what we know to be true in God's Word becomes our standard operating procedure, then what does or doesn't visibly happen is none of our business. Faithfulness is our sole responsibility; results are entirely God's.

In our case there were results, however, albeit not in the way we expected. They have come in the form of trust in our Beyond God like never before.

By definition trust means we believe our God knows best, and when His actions or timing do not match up with ours then we know He has a better plan and/or a reason beyond what we can comprehend with our limited brains. It's a matter of trusting a big, loving, sovereign God who is above and beyond us working His perfect plan.

When referring to the Old Testament patriarchs the writer to the Hebrews says it this way, "All these people were still living by faith when they died. They did not receive the things promised; they only saw them and welcomed them from a distance" (11:13).

Is it too crazy to believe that sometimes our level of trust is revealed more by what we don't presently see, than what we do? Do we still believe in, have faith in, trust in God when things don't go according to the way we think they should? Can we be content with the fact that God will be God no matter how much we don't understand or see outward evidence?

> Now faith is the assurance (title deed, confirmation) of things hoped for (divinely guaranteed), and the evidence of things not seen [the conviction of their reality—faith comprehends as fact what cannot be experienced by the physical senses]. For by this [kind of] faith the men of old gained [divine] approval. (Hebrews 11:1,2 AMP)

A major test of authentic faith is to trust our Father God, Who is close by, for the best things that will come in the future, even beyond our lifetime.

It's that "evidence of things not seen" thing that's the challenge to our human psyche, but that's precisely where trust keeps us sane.

## CHAPTER 14

# Unity, Not Uniformity

G od highly values unity. Although God created each of us as very unique with various personalities, spiritual gifts, talents and abilities, He has also called us to work together. He even commands it. As far as I can tell, the only thing God calls us to be totally independent from is sin. Outside of this, God instructs us not to be independent, but rather *interdependent* on one another by valuing each other's strengths and differences.

> Two are better than one, because they have a good return for their labor: If either of them falls down, one can help the other up, but pity anyone who falls and has no one to help them up. Also, if two lie down together, they will keep warm. But how can one keep warm alone? And if someone overpowers one person, two can resist him. A cord of three

strands is not easily broken. (Ecclesiastes 4:12 HCSB)

Just as a body, though one, has many parts, but all its many parts form one body, so it is with Christ...Now you are the body of Christ, and each one of you is a part of it. (I Corinthians 12:12, 27 NIV)

And He personally gave some to be apostles, some prophets, some evangelists, some pastors and teachers, for the training of the saints in the work of ministry, to build up the body of Christ, until we all reach unity in the faith and in the knowledge of God's Son, growing into a mature man with a stature measured by Christ's fullness. (Ephesians 4:11-13 HCSB)

Though most of us are familiar with these passages and hear them preached often, there are problems in the church because we fail to recognize that differences between individuals, while very challenging at times, can also be very good. We know that tests to good relationships in Christian circles are caused by more forces than disunity alone, but it's important to realize that conflict is one of Satan's biggest ploys when it comes to causing distraction and disruption in churches, ministries, or any other group, Christian or not.

I am convinced that nearly any issue can be resolved if God's people are willing to humble themselves, seek God's heart, and be willing to "speak the truth in love," which is the basis of true communication. As I have emphasized in pre-marital counseling over the years, loving communication is learning to listen to the heart of the other person in spite of the words. Sometimes our emotions get in the way of true communication. Other times it's pride. Often, it's both. If we really listen, we just may find we're not as far away from each other as we thought.

I am a realist. I know sometimes two parties encounter an impasse and must go different ways. We see it occurring between people and groups in the Bible. However, according to Scripture, unity of His people is near and dear to the heart of God.

The key to keeping our differences in proper perspective and preserving unity is found via a man who found himself writing from behind bars.

> Do nothing out of selfish ambition or vain conceit. Rather, in humility value others above yourselves, not looking to your own interests but each of you to the interests of the others. In your relationships with one another, have the same mindset as Christ Jesus: Who, being in very nature God, did not consider equality with God something to be used to his own advantage; rather, he made himself nothing by taking the very nature of a servant, being made in human likeness. And being found in appearance as a man, he humbled himself by becoming obedient to death—even death on a cross! (Philippians 2:3-8 )

Since we are attempting to view life through the lens of our Beyond God, it's only fitting we see what unity really looks like through the heart and mind of Jesus. The Apostle Paul could find no greater illustration than God's Son to paint this picture clearly. Truth is, Jesus is not only our best example, but the very means to unity created and cemented by humble love.

When it comes to living the abundant life and advancing God's kingdom, it's pretty obvious we are better together!

## Chapter 15

# "To our neighborhood, and beyond!"

Neither do we go beyond our limits by boasting of work done by others. Our hope is that, as your faith continues to grow, our sphere of activity among you will greatly expand, so that we can preach the gospel in the regions beyond you. For we do not want to boast about work already done in someone else's territory. (II Corinthians 10:15-16)

Paul's statement "beyond our limits" in verse 15 is in reference to his boasting, not his ministry. In fact, verse 16 is underscoring his (and God's) great desire to keep spreading the gospel so that "our sphere of activity among you will greatly expand, so that we can preach in the regions beyond you."

Paul never became satisfied with where he had been and how many disciples were made. Even though he rejoiced in the results, his desire was for the whole world to come to know Christ and he would do everything he could toward this end until his graduation to heaven. Paul's words and works declare he labored for a God who performed "above and beyond" mere human limits.

John Wesley carried a similar mantle as he once declared, "The World is my parish." It is never enough to keep the Christian message within the confines of the Christian community only. Reminding ourselves of the Great Commission's "beyond" terminology in Matthew 28:19, Mark 16:15, Luke 24:47, John 20:21 and Acts 1:8 is more than simple proof-texting, it's God's call to do more than we thought we could.

## CHAPTER 16

# Your Personal Beyond

None of what's been discussed does us any good, myself included, unless we're willing to put feet to our faith. Being a doer of the Word requires we make some important decisions then follow with action.

Asking the right questions is a good way to sweep away the debris so our heart has an easier time seeing what we need to do. The following are a few suggestions to help get the pump of our motivation primed.

What does your "beyond" look like?

- Has God been knocking on your heart's door urging you to get beyond your sin, yourself, and your purposeless life? Answer the door!

- Is your view of God too small? In other words, in your faith and thinking, have you allowed for the possibility that God can work in a way He's never done before if He wants, and He may even want to include you in this?

- What has God been asking you to do that you have been procrastinating?

- What habit or addiction (even a secret one) might you have that's been holding you back from becoming the person God has destined you to be?

- What vision did God plant inside you many years ago that you have shunned because of fear, finances or fickle people, yet it refuses to let you go?

- Are you harboring unforgiveness toward others, causing a hard heart and the inability to hear God clearly?

- Is your church, ministry, or organization floundering because the focus has been solely on what *has* worked instead of what *could* work?

- Is your main question always "Why?" instead of "Why not?"

- Has the progress of fulfilling your God-given vision slowed because your focus has become too narrow due to not recognizing the fact God frequently changes His methods of getting something done?

- Are you afraid of change? (As much as we say we want it, most of us resist it.)

- Are you afraid of failure? (Past disappointments can paralyze us if we're not careful.)

- Are you afraid of success? (This is not as crazy as it sounds.)

- Are you afraid of people? (Fear people or fear God, it's your choice.)

- Are you afraid? (Faith and fear do not mix. Perfect love is the antidote – 1 John 4:18.)

We must face the fact that, by nature, most of us generally resist change for various reasons. This requires we accept that meaningful modifications or improvements, to say nothing of brand new ideas, often won't be easy. Yet even here, especially here, God provides what we need to move forward "according to the power that works in us."

## CHAPTER 17

# The Family Picture

If we find it hard to do things differently as an individual, imagine multiplying that by the number of people in a particular church, ministry, or organization. This is precisely where allowing the nature of Jesus in us to control us comes into play big time. For the Christian, it's about both the end and the means. It's not just about what we accomplish, but how we accomplish it. While we're all familiar with the "Hatfields and McCoys" scenario, when it comes to nonessentials, God's people shouldn't disown a family member simply because we view situations differently or prefer to do things in another way.

If we implement changes but are leaving a long trail of spiritually or emotionally injured people along the way, then this may indicate we're not doing things the way Jesus would. However, we must also recognize some people will never accept certain kinds of change for a variety of reasons. There will always be people who resist no matter how great the idea, how effective the ministry, how needed the change is, or gifted the decision-makers are. It's worth noting that even some of Jesus' disciples stopped following him when they thought it was too hard or couldn't fully accept the new teaching Jesus was sharing. (John 6:60-69)

While the purpose of this book is not an in-depth study on communication theory or mass-marketing I believe it's worthwhile to refer to a landmark book written many years ago that addresses, in a practical way, how we are all different (by God's design!), and how this affects our approach to change. It was originally published in 1962 and has been revised 4 times, the latest being 2003.

In his book, Diffusion of Innovations, sociologist Everett Rogers highlighted five basic types of people based on their willingness to try out a new innovation or new product. He called these "adopter categories" and this concept is still used in present-day marketing. They are described as follows and illustrated by the graph below:

> *Innovators* make up 2.5 % of people in a group and are eager to try new ideas and are willing to take the risks necessary to get something new off the ground or make major changes. Others often see these as rash or daring.

*Early Adopters* make up 13.5 % of people and are generally respected by their peers. They have influence in their opinions with others in the larger group and are willing to give advice when asked.

*Early Majority* make up 34% of people and will accept new ideas just before the average person in the group they're a part of. While these will not usually be in leadership positions they play a major role in influencing others who are slower to get onboard.

*Late Majority* make up another 34% and are generally skeptical of anything new or different. They will come around only after most others have gotten onboard and a longer period of time has proven to them the idea is important and/or necessary.

*Laggards* make up the final 16% and are considered traditionalists and the last to adopt anything. They are preoccupied with the past, feeling all decisions must be made relative to previous generations, and find it next to impossible to think "out of the box."

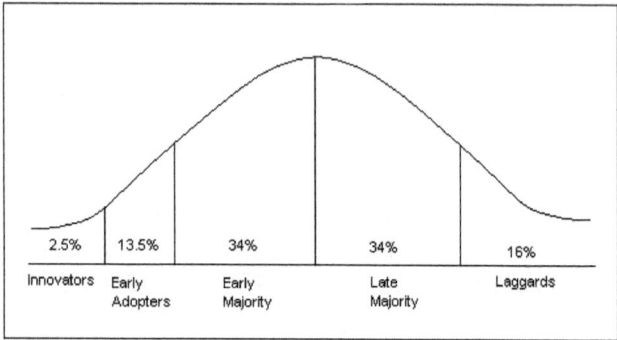

(*Diffusion of Innovations,* by Everett M. Rogers, Copyright 1995, 2003 by Everett M. Rogers / Copyright 1962, 1971, 1983 by The Free Press, A division of Simon and Shuster, Inc.)

The point is, in order to move forward, we must take advantage (in the best sense of this word) of the people God has placed around us. We are not to step on them or manipulate them, but honestly respect others as the unique and gifted creation of God they are. Obviously, the first call of every person is to know God and keep growing in that knowledge, but we must also know others as well as our self. Without good relationships, we're all but dead in the water. Making efforts at moving forward becomes a waste of energy if the two people in the canoe are paddling in opposite directions. Taking the same scenario, if both are paddling in the same direction progress is made, even if their style of how they paddle differs.

Though this all sounds good, what do we do when a vision is revealed but an "innovator" is locking horns with a "late majority" person, or a "laggard" is getting frustrated with an "early adopter"? Realistically, any big undertaking requiring the cooperation of a number of people will likely never have one hundred percent acceptance this side of heaven. This means we must look beyond our present limitations and frustrations to the Beyond God within us.

> Therefore, if you have any encouragement from being united with Christ, if any comfort from his love, if any common sharing in the Spirit, if any tenderness and compassion, then make my joy complete by being like-minded, having the same love, being one in spirit and of one mind. Do nothing out of selfish ambition or vain conceit. Rather, in humility value others above yourselves, not looking to your own interests but each of you to the interests of the others. In your relationships with one another, have the same mindset as Christ Jesus... (Philippians 2:1-5)

Any vision or call that is truly from God must move forward according to His leading, but God's Word requires we do so with a Christlike attitude along the way. We must plainly understand there will always be nay-sayers, or worse. This does not mean we run roughshod over them, but show grace to them as God has poured out grace upon us. There will be many occasions when "speaking the truth in love" (Ephesians 4:15) needs to happen, but we must double-check ourselves to make sure it's love doing the talking. As you may have heard: "Truth without love is brutal, but love without truth is hypocritical". There is always a need for both love and firmness in pursuing the vision.

## CHAPTER 18

# Who's in us?

All that God is He is in His names, and all
that He is in His names He was in Christ. All
that He is in Christ, He is in us! (Jack Taylor)

For the entire fullness of God's nature dwells
bodily in Christ, and you have been filled by
Him, who is the head over every ruler and
authority. (Colossians 2:9-10)

The greatest hindrance to almost every Christian
I know (including me) is that we don't have a
full, proper understanding of Who is in us and all
this means. This holds us back. It cripples us in our
thinking and stifles our growth as a Christian. Our
limited understanding of the purpose and power of
Jesus Christ in us causes us to be spiritually anemic.
If we only knew what potential we have beyond our

human limitations I believe both our courage and our effectiveness would increase exponentially! I have experienced it in myself and witnessed it in others.

God's Word shouts down through the ages that our mighty God continues to administrate the universe from beyond the reaches of the farthest galaxy and everywhere in between, while also living inside of every true believer. He chose to live inside us in spite of us. The question then becomes, are we willing to grasp all this means:

> …that our limitations no longer disqualify us from serving God,

> …that we have a God-given purpose to fulfill,

> …that we have authority over the powers of darkness that try to hinder us at every turn,

> …that we can beat temptation every time,

> …that God has called us to live beyond the mere human level to the higher dimension Jesus lived in by the power of the Holy Spirit?

So, the next time someone recognizes God worked a miracle through us, or thanks us for sharing His love through an act of kindness, or appreciates that we communicated the truth of the unchanging Word of God, or we see God doing some amazing things through our church or ministry, we can honestly say, "Thank Jesus, because it's beyond me!"

> My response is to get down on my knees before the Father, this magnificent Father who parcels out all heaven and earth. I

ask him to strengthen you by his Spirit—not a brute strength but a glorious inner strength—that Christ will live in you as you open the door and invite him in. And I ask him that with both feet planted firmly on love, you'll be able to take in with all followers of Jesus the extravagant dimensions of Christ's love. Reach out and experience the breadth! Test its length! Plumb the depths! Rise to the heights! Live full lives, full in the fullness of God.

God can do anything, you know—far more than you could ever imagine or guess or request in your wildest dreams! He does it not by pushing us around but by working within us, his Spirit deeply and gently within us.

Glory to God in the church!
Glory to God in the Messiah, in Jesus!
Glory down all the generations!
Glory through all millennia! Oh, yes!
(Ephesians 3:16-21 MSG)

# CHAPTER 19

# LIVING BEYOND

There's a stirring throughout the cosmos one night,
Yahweh stood o'er His majestic domain.
His grand design for the universe, ready to unfold,
a masterplan where He'd eternally reign.
Rumbles resound and as the Father says the Word,
a sphere appears from the vacuum of space.
Yahweh's Spirit comes forth hove'ring over this globe,
earth is born and there's a smile on His face.
As the commands continue, creation obeys His lead,
even time joins this celestial parade.
The Word's there, too, making intricate things,
without Him nothing was made that was made.
Then comes the moment when all creation holds still,
the Father stoops down in the sand.
He's really in no hurry, as He forms a certain shape,
then breathes His own life into man.

Soon a serpent appears in this garden serene,
approaching Eve with his deceitful confusion.
It was just one bite, but that's all that it took,
so began sin's relentless infusion.
But all was not lost, Yahweh always has a plan,
He would get us beyond sin's clutch.
He would do what it took, for He's gracious that way,
our Beyond God loves us so much.
It was the Word once again, that created our light,
paid the price sin rightfully demanded.
By faith we're set free from the darkness within us,
it was life that He firmly commanded.
But our God wasn't done, nor will He ever be,
He provides us power beyond our need.
Our limitations would never again hold us back,
we can follow where'er He will lead.
So, please don't be fooled by Satan's slick ways,
for so many are easily conned.
We can do more, much more, for eternity's sake,
if we'll focus on our God who's beyond!

# About the Author

Rev. Brian Sharp has been involved in ministry for over forty years, and at his present church for twenty-four of those. In addition to pastoring, he is involved with several outreach ministries in his community including addiction recovery, jail ministry, and food distribution to the needy. He is ordained with and serves on the Executive Board of World Ministry Fellowship based in Plano, Texas. He is a graduate of Oral Roberts University, and Perkins School of Theology, Southern Methodist University. While Brian totally loves his family, enjoys writing, delights in photography, and is mesmerized by God's great universe, his greatest desire is to see believers wholeheartedly love Jesus and serve Him in the power of the Holy Spirit.

He and Pam, his bride of thirty-nine years, met in the cafeteria at ORU and now pastor Grace Christian Fellowship, Poplar Bluff, Missouri. They have three grown children – Naomi Lives in Missouri, Breanne lives in Colorado, and Stephanie lives in heaven. If you'd like to contact Brian please go to gcfpb.com.

Address: 1391 County Road 607, Poplar Bluff, Missouri, 63901.

Email: blsharp72@gmail.com

Phone: (573) 429-8479

www.ingramcontent.com/pod-product-compliance
Lightning Source LLC
La Vergne TN
LVHW021611080426
835510LV00019B/2515